Made in the USA
Middletown, DE
12 August 2021

45894516R00194